IN A PREDICAMENT ALL MY LIFE
(A Collection of Poems)

Prudentia Binwi Asobo

Langaa Research & Publishing CIG
Mankon, Bamenda

Publisher:
Langaa RPCIG
Langaa Research & Publishing Common Initiative Group
P.O. Box 902 Mankon
Bamenda
North West Region
Cameroon
Langaagrp@gmail.com
www.langaa-rpcig.net

Distributed in and outside N. America by African Books Collective
orders@africanbookscollective.com
www.africanbookscollective.com

ISBN: 9956-762-88-1

DISCLAIMER
All views expressed in this publication are those of the author and do
not necessarily reflect the views of Langaa RPCIG.

Table of Contents

Alengnge nifor (The Royal Stool)

A protest raged on a palace lawn,
Round a makeshift stage Princes charged on,
Fifteen and more they say,
Seize the stool that day
A Prince held up *alengne nifor*,
Cursed it, and called it a dirty chair.

An elderly man pushed through the fuming multitude,
With a corroded shotgun shouldered proud.
His '*Thogrie*' (Traditional regalia) was old and washed-out,
He had polished his shoes shiny and bright.
He crossed that stage with a *nku'um's* (palace guard) grace,
Until he and the Prince stood face to face.

Liberty of words the elderly man whispered,
Is worth dying for, good men are dead,
So you can stand on this palace lawn,
And talk to us down from dusk to dawn.
But before any stool gets carried away today,
This old man is going to have his say!

My father's corpse is on a foreign land,
For the reason that they said would end all conflict.
But Amadou and I wasn't even full grown,
Before we fought in a war of our own.
As Alahaji died without a word,
In the shadow of a palace he once build.

Where good men fight over *alenge nifor*,
Raising their voices loud and high

The Princes lift his scepter high
His royal garment high
His feathered cap highest
That the whole world could see it fly!

I got this half arm that I still drag,
Fighting for this same old stool.
The black beret boys and girls chopped off my arm
As I fight to throw back tear-gas
Held 'grenete' hard in my palm
Booooom! It chopped off my arm

Now this riot never came to pass.
The crowd got quiet and that can of gas,
Got set aside as they walked away
To talk about what they had done this day.
Now there's but one arm on my thorax,
You'll burn in hell for my arm's sake.

So now it's time to decide which road to take,
Which one of you will follow our lead,
To stand and die for what you believe,
For as sure as there is a rising sun,
We'll follow its rays
And God knows our course is just.

As a shadow all my life

Fifty years plus
I walk as a shadow
Fifty years plus
I walk behind
Fifty years plus
I am a silent listener
Fifty years plus
I am a decision taker

Years past,
My situation remains
Years past,
I walk as a shadow
All my life I'm behind
Always walking
One step behind,
And things have not changed

As I'm standing here,
I don't know what to do
When they move I move
When they stand I stand
Even though I want to run
I cannot run and I'm afraid
Because I'm walking as a shadow
Where ever they moved, I moved

Though I walk as a shadow,
I need someone who is like me
Someone who is like me from within

Someone who looks the same way
Someone who sounds like me
Another that has the same composure
Another that walks as a shadow
So when we pray I'll confide in him about my shame.

Will I live as a shadow all my life?
I ran when they ran
I sang *cher patrie*, when they sing
I hum when they hum
I'm only seen when the sun is up
When heaven sheds tears, I'm not noticed
If I was to be granted any wish
I would want to walk alone

As A Suspect All My Life

I've been a slave for fifty years plus
I was always right there
Holding onto their three piece suits
While my *thogrie* (traditional regalia) crawls in mud.
For long ago, I had met my waterloo
Now I know I am a stranger
When leave to my chamber
I'll come back with a decicion.

When the moment comes
I will record all that I hear,
Please sing good music
Speak good language
That would tell me I'm loved
Give me silence to absorb my ears
And I will perceive all you say
I am waiting patiently to move besides you

I understand more rapidly
Than you would imagine.
I would not speak French to you
I might not be Napoleon's grandson,
Please understand, I am human.
I would not stop you,
Please do not be misled by my silence
And I'll make imprints of your journey

The End Shall Come

I know my people, and my people know me,
Though with depressing and wrinkled faces,
When I wave my flag, they column after me,
Their outer emergence is numerous,
My instincts tell me, the end shall come.

When I lean on their shoulders,
Crying for help,
They clean my tears,
They calm my fret,
And say, the end shall come.

Illegitimacy and dishonesty looms,
Promises, easier said than done,
No pipe born water, no good roads,
No hospitals, limited schools, no electricity,
Yet we applaud and appreciate?

Half a century ago,
We've been hijacked by pirates,
They've eaten until throwing up,
Fighting among themselves,
And that we know the end shall come.

The Moungo Randez-vous

Did you preach unity?
Alone I cry out my sadness
Alone I voice out my fears.
Alone I try to understand,
Alone, I seek knowledge.
Yet you call make me a fool.

When I was in diapers,
His people brought gifts,
Palm wine in calabashes
Achu in basins
Palm oil in tins
And kola nut in *akikag* (bamboo basket)

Shaking the *nka'a-mu* (locally made lamp) till it burns to ashes
They lighted my neighbourhood
They warmed my village
My people danced
My people ululated
A mbue eweloo? (in whose house)

I was engaged
He said we are indivisible
we go tok one tok
we go put we money for one goo'goong
me and you na finger and nail
ma family na ya own .

My smile brightened his day
I massaged his back when it ached

7

I graced his bed
My breasts his pillows
My tongue his sweet
Yet he calls me a fool

Our rendez-vous was at the Moungo
Two parts of the same 'world'
When I fell for him
He distracted me from my Biafra man,
Filled my ears with marriage talks,
I thought marriage was a bed of roses.

When the morning sun rose
I was there earlier than him
I watched the dry petals flood on the sea
I watched the canoe men paddle
I watched the birds hop
Skipping from branch to branch

He pointed to the left and to the right.
This is former Southern Cameroon
This is Former French Cameroon
They tied the knot here.
This river binds them together.
Can we do as they did in 1961?

My parents didn't school me about marriage.
I signed papers I did not read.
Decisions were already made
I signed my own death warrant,
I ticked "Yes", I fell in love blindly
Now, I stew in my stew.

My future 'hambugs' me
My hair itches as though I have lice.
Can Achu be replaced with cassava?
Can Achu soup become Ndole?
Can we replace Achu with o'kok?
Can "I tok say" be "je dit que"?

All day long, my heart bleeds.
He let me down so soon,
He calls me a fool
Where is that lovely smile?
What happened to our embrace at the Moungo?
I have to open a search.

Mengie-Ntoh (Queen Mother)

I've gone through all
The night was dark
Distant and remote
I wonder what lured me to *ntoh*
Traditional curiosity perhaps
An eagerness to sell my culture
To learn more about my culture
My barbaric cultures as the red men say

Let me tell you my ordeal in *awandu*
I was dressed in the red *awand*,
An almost red *Gigidja'a* around me
My forehead of coweries
My figure eight well exposed
Tensed with anxiety to move
But a strange voice howled
And whispered my name sharply.

Mengie-ntoh, mengie-ntoh, mengie-ntoh (Queen Mother)
Hey, hey there…stop, stop
Stop that barbaric dance
I turned around and shaked like *antchinie* (traditional meat)
I had a drink of palm wine
But felt no better
Taking *mentchin-ntoh's* (Palace guard) hand in mine
We went down into the palace

I saw the figure in silhouette
His tone was nasty
And *mentchin-ntoh* (Palace guard) whispered

10

Perhaps he's come to stop *ilere* (annual dance)
Their men asked us not to fire guns
We listened and obeyed
Why are they here again?
Should we continue to obey?

I have my bow and arrow here
I'll not run, I'll not sell my culture
I grew up in this tradition
I would die because of it
I've got my bow and arrow ready.
Thwack, thwack, thwack
He got his gun ready too
But *Mbeh* (His magesty)roared and retorted.

Once upon a time

Once upon a time,
An awful culture settled amongst us,
They schooled us in their ways,
Coated our fingers nails with nail polish,
Forced us to eat with spoons,
Their plates replaced our plantain leaves,
Salad and hamburger were served,
And *achu* (traditional meal) thrown into dust bins.

Terror ran through spines,
As they destroyed our *itushies* (ancestral shrines)
Cruel and imposing,
Sermonizing about their God,
This colonial mentality,
Our pale faces depict pity provoked,
All in the name of civilisation,
And we snooze in boredom

Lack of intellectualism in our culture,
An agonizing religion,
Planted at the helm of our states,
An image of a bleak future,
Forever making us infantile,
And as true as anything else,
Society relies on those that are advanced,
Captivated by their new technology and sciences

They destroy the framework of society,
Using rationalistic methods,
Major malaise of humanity.

Shall we listen to them?
Society's democracy is irrelevant,
We're sick and tired of it,
And this is a painful truth,
For it's just colonialism continuing.

Society needs creative thinkers,
Society needs committed leaders,
Who'll inspire people to work?
Institute a standard of distinction,
Vision inspirers for citizens to excel,
To make dreams come true,
And not a culture of intellectual laziness,

We must not implant another dictator,
But one who'll set accountability structures,
Conduit the present to bottomless pits,
Surpass the status quo,
Work with imagination, insight, and boldness,
Bring in innovative lay down of hope,
And initiate standards of excellence.

Awoundo Gigidja'a

As the sun opened its bright eye,
The gloomy eye of darkness closing,
We open our tearful eyes,
 Releasing a film of oozing tears,
And watch it crawl on weary cheeks.

They negotiated this identity,
Marketed us in 1961,
Sadness weighed on us,
In that Foumban stronghold,
As they were given bleak options.

Assimilationists French did this,
Its ugly temper bearing on us,
Scrapping off who we are,
Twisting our tongues on *parlez, parlez*,
And it is why I will not hide my woes.

How shall I keep my *awondo* and *gigidja*?
How shall I hold on to my *thogrie*?
So that it does not touch their bow ties?
How shall I lift it gently over?
So that it doesn't rub in mud?

Should I tuck it away?
Among long forgotten objects in the trunks?
Amongst the ancestral heads?
In the camwood and coweries
In some quiet unknown place, somewhere
To avoid their perfumed bow ties?

Should I tie it in plantain leaves?

Alu'ungi (Dirge)

Flies would join the mourners too
In a weak faculty of utterance
He shook like a leaf
At his blame of eternal rule;
His words rebel his appearance
Plein des grandes ambitions
Full of wisdom and of assurance
My dear neighbour
Then I laugh myself to derision
Because I knew he would speak.

Nemesis would meet them
They might sing the songs of 'renouveau'
Great aspiration lyrics
But when their pulse stops
When thunder storms rumble
When lightning strikes them
When nimbus clouds fill the air
When the sky turns grey
And heaven's tears drop
Not even their armed thugs would save them

The Walk to Foumban

In a slow
Yet silent walk to Foumban,
Anglophone brains silently move,
Would "mount" the stage,
Arms set akimbo,
Like Johnny's "anointed successors,"
I pray to watch his footsteps
And make their voices heard.

Poised with some traces
Of Johnny's thoughts,
That runs in blood
And down Palace walls,
Rubbed with reserves of Johnny's midnight oils,
Ready to break through barriers,
Build the society he envisaged,
Giving back to the community what it needs

Proud country men of John Ngu Foncha,
Vulnerable children need warmth,
Their pain is your pain,
Do you hear them
When they cry for help?
Under bridges, some lay their heads,
So young, helpless, poor and weak in heart,
Yet we send motions of support.

The Bartered Citizen

Sure, call me any horrible name you choose,
The ugly name does not stain.
I am the poor Anglo-fool,
Fooled and pushed apart.
I am like a slave bearing drudger scars.
Submitting to a dominating influence,
And finding only the same old stupid culture.

I am the Anglo-fool driven from the land.
I am the young Anglo-fool, full of strength and hope.
I am the Anglo-fool clutching the hope I seek,
But tangled in that ancient endless chain,
Forced to move like that ancient slave,
And so my fist is clenched,
Determined to take back my freedom again.

It's a shame!
I am the Anglo-fool, belittled.
I am the Anglo-fool sold to the French.
I am the Anglo-fool, servant to Franco-frogs.
Owning everything for your own greed?
The bartered citizen throughout the years?
Yet I'm one of those who dreamt our indispensable dream?

I am the man who never gets ahead.
Oh! I'm the man who sailed those early seas in the Biafra,
In search of what I meant to be my independence.
With my bricks and stones, I gave a helping hand,
To build a "free Cameroon."
I am one of them that dreamt a dream so strong,

So brave, so true
Yet I am a nobody?

No way to Hide

Up the lifters,
Bossing and booing,
Now down,
Silent and mute,
Biggie's big eye
Caught them,
And there was no way to hide.

From a curious crowd
He pointed them,
Surrounded by penitentiaries,
Memorizing Bigge's orders,
No shaking,
"You shake I shoot"
And there was no way to hide.

In sunken jaws,
Steeping down
From heavily guarded truck,
I duck my head down,
For fear our sight might meet,
These were the very thugs
From whom I suffered torture.

From grace to grass,
In moments of weariness
And heart pain,
With tranquil sorrow in handcuffs,
Opposing those moments
 Of ululation,

And of cheers in fur seats

Now in shame
Now in humiliation,
Gently led by pistol men
To magistrates,
Protruding bellies
Now pressed to backbones,
Void of *le Vin de Paris*

Fallen jaws
Wrinkled faces,
In whose bodies
Misery abides,
Drinking tear,
Almost half death in spirit,
Even *le vin de palm* too is absent.

As they stepped
Into the courtyard,
We see sorrowing manifesting.
Did they touch Biggie's currency?
But they must sleep in that cubicle
It's biggie's decision.

Let us become we

Let us together, say:
"You are my brother,
Anglophone or Francophone.
Let us become instead we,
One single hand
That can united rise,
To smash the old dead
Dogmas of the past,

Kill the lies of culture,
That keep the rich enthroned,
Driving our youths to scamming
To 419,
Helpless, stupid, and scattered.
Brother against brother,
Because one is Anglophone,
Another Francophone.

You are my sister-now-today!
Let's develop the land that is ours.
The mines
And the factories ,
At Loumpanga,
Bam et kim,
Let the plants
The roads

Let the tools of power be ours.
For me, no more,

Anglophone Francophone Phenomenon.
Let us forget what the imperialist brought,
Let us learn new lessons,
Make new life-ways,
Form a new union
Until the future burns out every past mistake.

Liberty Fighters

In this peaceful realm,
From the fountains of a peaceful past,
We drowned in the flow of peace,
And redeem evil by a regained ecstasy,
Only in this once peaceful realm we found calm,
For the sharp intellect of man.

Praise the libertyfighters,
Praise Nelson Mandela,
Praise Nkwame Nkrumah,
Praise Ngu Foncha,
You departed from this paradise ,
Now made worthless and insignificant.

With their morning mist, fruitfulness came.
With their evening cloud affluence came.
In this once peaceful realm,
They projected themselves as a rock of defence.
In the garden of their minds, peace was rooted,
And defence for human nature was their itinerary.

Like upholders and preservers,
Carrying with them love and loves,
They immeasurable quest for salvation,
In ambivalence and fantasy,
Especially to the contemporary man,
In this once peaceful realm.

My ancestors, strengthen me,
Even in my slumber I hear them speak?

24

And the music that flowed from their lips,
And cause me sing a lullaby?
I'll sing a lullaby I heard my mothers sang
To bring their babes to sleep

Let your light shine and shine upon us,
As we faint in darkness.
Plant a pillar of florescent bulbs on our walls,
That it might flash the eyes of demons,
Those stand by my door,
And paralyse their wicked assignments.

Opponents in the house

Once,
I fell in a waterway,
I heard the mountains
Singing his surname
Frogs of the valley croak his Christian name,
Birds of the hill sang his given name,
Yet she seats unperturbed.

The winds of the sphere whisper it,
The endless plains
Sing his family name
Doomed in company
With throbbing doubts,
They are traitors
Enemies in the house.

Shall it be the same?
On judgement day?
He's in trepidation
And desolation,
The ministerial folk misinform him,
In desperate need of light,
He protests in ignorance of her people.

I should wish
she finds contentment,
In prime care arise and glow,
Subdue his horrific mind's eye,
And turn her woes
to glorious gain,

That her path might glimmer.

Lend a hand
Of reconstruction Lord,
Put together her wits
Holy One,
Refurbish ecstasy of resurgence in her
And revolve heartache to splendour,
Upon the path that pleases her.

Reassemble a future for us,
Let luminosity gleam
And excel again,
That she might take that direction,
Whose high enterprise we desire,
Else we fall
In that colonial pit again.

Rats That Bite And Blow

My days we knew not these
The truth shall hunt them
Deceased shadows must hunt them
Ah! Bitter, bitter world
This political pandemonium?
Uncompromising relationships
Be wise, think deeply
Rats that bite and blow?
Rat poisons must be made available
Then I'll enshrine the past
For future restoration

I see you at the edge of rot
You and your white-skinned men
You and your long nose brothers in crime.
Camwood men won't move
When the alu'ungi drums shall sound
When the choristers raise their voices
When they move their lungs, larynx and syrinx
Shadows of death shall pursue you
And that would be an end to tyranny.

Beacons of Cameroon

In this Cameroon,
In this land of John Ngu Foncha,
That Bamenda man with cap and feather?
Yes, that proud Anglophone Cameroonian,
That Beacon of Cameroon,
Who in the speechless sorrow of his eyes,
Head off the Camera's *petit* eyeball.

In this Cameroon,
I'll take out my drums,
I'll take out my calabash,
I'll bring palm wine and kola nuts,
I'll bring palm oil and Camwood,
Rub it on your now bony cheeks,
To let it hide your unpleasant tears.

In this Cameroon,
I'll support your head with my regalia,
My Bamenda tőghe,
Then I'll bring the nkeng leaves,
And lay down at your feet,
All the soft things,
And repose your gentle spirit.

Because my mouth is wide with laughter,
Because my feet are gay with dancing,
My throat itchy with praise songs,
I'll sing a lullaby,

I'll sing the twin songs too,
For your peaceful repose,
And I hope you'll hear it.

In this Cameroon,
I'll make my voice heard,
I'll share my thoughts with everyone,
In my fingertips I feel your thoughts,
With my pen, paper, ink and eraser,
I'll shape my thoughts into words,
And I pray my pen shall not run short of ink.

In this Cameroon,
Land of great heroes,
The land harbouring John Fru Ndi,
The ever smiling ST Muna,
The stubborn AN Jua
The rattling N.N Mbile
The confident EML Endeley

This land of Green,
Red and Yellow,
The land
On which those feet
Of ancient time walked,
The land that bears
The weight of peace

The Godfathered

Blessed are the Godfathers,
For they give jobs to the unqualified.

Blessed are the politicians,
For they lie at election without fear.

Blessed are the Godfathered,
For they have tickets.

Blessed are the Magistrates,
For they will dodge anything.

Blessed are the khaki boys and girls,
For their pay vouchers are heavy.

Blessed are the red beret boys and girls,
For they receive high vouchers after a riot.

Blessed are their children,
No one can control their spending.

Blessed are the foreign banks,
For they safeguard their booty.

Blessed are the Church Ministers,
They preach good news to the poverty-stricken.

Frailty

This is my worry
Thought of bad
Becoming worse,
My heart leaps
I looked around me,
I looked ahead of me,
And I looked behind me.

A society void of harmony
Bound Centre, North, West, South,
East, North West
And South West
By natural piety
Was it like that when I was born?
Shall it be the same when I'm a woman?

Ah! Wish I wasn't born there
I'm a happy woman,
Praying for freedom
The freedom of the individual mind
To look through all the frailties of my world
One devoid of harmony
And therefore bound to think

I reflect society's wellbeing
Plagued by violence
The mountains
And the endless plain stink of it
Brother talks ill of brothers
A brother kills brethren

Yet goes with impunity

They're all inquisitive

The whole creation groans,
Patiently waiting for that great day,
Yet struggle with the pangs of corruption,
Of redemption, and adoption

Around the swampy river side,
Skipping from one pond to another,
Frogs of the valley croak,
Humans too groan, within themselves.

Croaking in joy with lofty thoughts,
Not to be overwhelmed,
By the toothless bulldog,
Not even the lion that roars.

In that great valley within their dwell,
Solitude, fear or grief, may not be their passion,
The green shrubs shed their bed,
Yet they get ready to sleep.

They're all inquisitive,
Shall their wellbeing change?
Who shall bring this change?
And the thought of liberty overwhelms.

In those pleasant still waters,
They moan and whinge,
Knowing nature hates them,
But God's elect shall come and rescue them.

Let Cameroon be Cameroon Again

Cameroon is not Cameroon to me.
On the lookout for cultural sustenance,
Let Cameroon be Cameroon again.
Let it be the image it used to be.
Let it be the lead the way in West Africa,
That no man be crushed by another.

We've become toddlers
Crying babies of the world?
The most breast fed babies of the world.
Our hands always long-drawn-out out,
Stretched out, lengthened
Begging for salvation.

We are victims of circumstances
Our forefathers did this.
They brought us into it.
They contracted an incompatible marriage
They failed to keep their marriage vows
And lived as two rather than one.

Let Cameroon be Cameroon again,
Let Cameroon be the dream the dreamers dreamed,
Let it be that great strong land of love,
No conspiracy crawling
Nor oppressors' intrigue.
For Cameroon is not Cameroon to me.

Never's been equality for me,
All I breathe is marginalisation.

O, let it be a land where independence is independence,
Where equality looms the air,
Not crowned with no false patriotic crowns.
One where opportunity is real and life free.

Ger-Bri-Fre rule

When I was a little girl,
My grand ma used to tell me,
She would recount her experiences with the Germans,
She would recount her melancholy under British rule,
She would tell me how she worked on their farms,
Tilling their soil from dawn to dusk.

They all packed their bags,
And we thought it's all over?
Here am I in the post German rule,
Here am I in the post British rule,
Here am I in the post French rule,
Here am I in the *Ger-Bri-Fre* rule again.

They quarrel me on daily basis,
They say I am that fool West of the Mongo.
They shout at me at the least offense,
They say I will never keep their funding,
Else I chop their wealth,
And expose their balance sheets to my foolish brothers.

When I asked them why?
They say I like to annoy them.
Where I belong, there is no joy,
They would say to my face:
Je n'ai jamais aimé les Anglophones.
Yet I love them unconditionally.

My handkerchiefs are dripping,
And my being is dreary.

This hatred blows me away,
When I think how they treat me.
When tears shade my sight, I ask:
Did grand pa fight that war of independence?
Did grandma join the *takumbeng* women?

The Germans did not know,
The British did not know,
The French did not know,
But now we know,
Yes we know,
The end shall come.
Shall bad governance end?

Sugar Coated Tongues

There is no dialogue in their democracy.
We hoped for economic freedom,
They brought flag freedom;
We hoped for political independence,
They brought flag independence,
Rendering us financially handicapped.

In their highly air conditioned offices,
Filled with hazardous ego,
They deceive the youths with currency,
Colonizing juvenile brains,
Involving innocent teenagers into war.
Divulging the immature hearts into crime.

They claim holiest than every other man
We are not intimidated by their speeches,
Speeches that have no traces of reality,
Most delicate, worse than mysterious,
Claiming innocence like toddlers,
Yet no body cautions them.

Walking in exhaustion and lack of stability,
Walking as though sleepy,
Unable to bear their own weight,
Supported by innocent thugs,
They mount the rostrum,
 Where invalid promises are made.

When they deceitfully say their minds,
They send thugs to burn our houses,

Burn their shrines and ancestral tombs,
Burn the women's market places,
Burn farmlands, cattle and pigs,
Failing in their duty as custodians of life.

Men that say no to tyranny yet perpetuate it?
Presenting images of terror before men,
With hopes dashed to disillusionment,
Men neglected by snobbery,
And in a tone deliberately low they moan
And I was tempted to ask: what manner of leaders are these?

As A Victim All My Life

I opened my eyes
Pondering.
Of what is life designed?
It was all colourless,
And soul jeopardizing.
Am I a victim as well?
Trying to escape victimhood?
That those i was thinking I recognize
Become 'hearsay' bearers?

With wrinkled eyes
With tearful eyes
I glanced into my mirror.
I see dishonesty
I see suppression
I see segregation
I see corruption manifest
I see murders
That we all have is to die?

My calabash clutched to my ribs
I looked around
To see the best river to fetch from
All I saw were foreign rivers.
So now, I must choose
To either escape or succumb.
Be on your highest alert dearest
One could be your closest friend
And ends you up bruised

What is drowning us?
It's time for a revolution,
Change of perception,
Change of mind-set,
Change of conduct
Let's get out of discomfort zones,
We need a change
Change for the better .
It's revolution time!!

Shall My People Be Like M'dela?

Lord, our dreams are dead.
Today, we are no longer one.
Clearly, we are more of babies,
That must take what is given us.
We choke in dangerous tear-gas
And poisonous smoke.
Uniform men pour water on us,
Water drained from toilets,
Land heavy whips on our backs,
To squash our demonstrations.

Social and economic malaise pervade society,
Depression and disrespect saturate the social order,
As many are shot down when we strike,
Many who knew not what was going on,
And I faint in anguish,
Seeing violent blows to humanity.
I was weak and weary,
When I held their cadaver,
And kissed their foreheads
To bid Goodbye to lifeless heroes.

On my psyche, sad words of melancholy appear,
Resenting images of misery float my mind.
Signs of impending doom bruise my imagination.
For all the dreams I dream,
Of all the rebellious songs I sing,
Of all the hopes I hold,
All the freedom flags I waved,
Matched from pillar to post,

All I have are hopeless dreams,
Dormant in bottomless pits.

Why are we trying to destroy each other?
Can my people be like M'dela?
He stood up for what is right,
M'dela I understand what you went through,
Today, your people reap what you sowed.
Lord, dedicate part of your time Lord,
Do something that will assist humanity,
Do something that can change life for the better.
Work selflessly and make this country a better place,
Different than that known to the outside world know.

Never Mind My Brother

Once blissful, becomes sour?
In every furrow I turned manure too
To fertilize the seeds we planted,
To make Cameroon the land what it has become.
Yet I am that underdog.
Akin to the he goat we stink?
That idiot from West Cameroon.

You confer on me severe whips?
You proffer me pitiable pay?
For honest thoughts, diligent works
You spit in my face?
And call me the idiot at reunification.
Yet I have the Idiotic hand in me
That foolish supply yet made Cameroon.

The Idiot whose sweat and blood,
Whose faith and pain,
Whose plow in the rain,
Produced the fruits you now consume?
Never mind my brother,
As slippery as the road might be,
We must bring back our mighty dream again.

Let's conduit the present to the future,
Surpass the status quo, bury intellectual laziness,
Bring in innovative lay downs of hope,
Set accountability structures
And initiate a standard of excellence.
Smash assimilation and readymade cultures;

The major malaise of our culture.

Big Brother's net

He pointed at them,
His net was ready,
From all corners of the of sea,
Big brother watched them,
Brother sounded a note of warning,
Had vaunted his claims,
And vowed he would pick them all,
He swore he would discharge all fraudulent men.

Pickpockets ignored him,
Go swimming in privileged circumstances,
Their balance sheets filled top to down,
Biggie didn't get on nerves
But continued to cast his net,
Like an egg shell he will crack up their coffers,
And play the game as Big Brother would,
Else his compatriots drag him in mud.

Alas! Big Brother's net caught them,
In all the might of their endeavour,
They were lost in the sea,
Caught in big brother's net,
Struggling to no avail,
To break through big brother's net,
With their hands in cuffs,
Like slaves of old in manacles.

Before them lay the emptiness of life,
No guards, no thugs,
To their prison cells,

They would march on,
Prison guards marched too,
Marching on like the slaves in the days past,
And Big brother would pack them,
In cold like fish in the coldest degree.

Society crafted it so

This is my worry,
My heart soars,
The thought of bad becoming worse,
My heart leaps awake,
As this stares roughly at me.

I looked to the lead of society,
I looked at the rear of it,
My eyes blur and ache,
In the face of confusion,
To look through all the frailties of his world.

I stare nakedly at his world,
I stroll'd back, and stroll'd forward,
And it's just as I see
Society crafted it so.
Was it like that when he was born?

I tasted here, and went through there,
Tasting here and there,
Requiring freedom of personality,
But my heart is of vague impression,
And can't verbalize encouraging words.

My belly rumbles, and my mind bleeds,
Society toasts me left and right,
Although I sob in recollection of my past,
I'll not judge by my past,
Even if I perceive my folks as traitors.

Once, I fell in a waterway,
The mountains sang his surname,
Frogs of the valley croak his Christian name,
Birds of the hill sang his given name,
Yet he seats still on that stool.

The winds of the sphere whisper it,
The endless plains sing his family name
He was doomed in company with throbbing doubts,
He sees his people as devils?
Les enemies dans la maison.

Shall it be the same on judgement day?
He's in trepidation and desolation,
The ministerial folk misinform him,
In desperate need of light,
He protests in ignorance of his people.

I should wish he finds contentment,
In prime care arise and glow,
Subdue his horrific mind's eye,
And turn his woes to glorious gain,
That his path might glimmer.

Lend a hand of reconstruction Lord,
Put together his wits Holy One,
Refurbish ecstasy of resurgence in him
And revolve heartache to splendour,
Upon the path that pleases him.

Reassemble a future for us,
Let luminosity gleam and excel again,

That he might take that direction,
Whose high enterprise we desire,
Else we fall in the colonial pit again.

Grand Camarad

Every day that passes,
Takes us down to the road,
We pray to one day dare say:
Yes this is the day,
The day we have been waiting for.

He didn't conduct elections,
Without delay,
He called Foncha up,
Yes! He did,
But he knows if people couldn't vote,
Stones would vote.

Endeley's grip on Foncha's hand was visible,
Sliding slowly, and patiently,
Liberating the praise-worthy seat
Peacefully,
Without unshackles or handcuffs.
What an example from Endeley?
.
Bro, sit here,
Endeley ordered.
Bring in new ideas,
Bring in Bamenda brains,
Bring the *thogrie* to limelight.

So too the authoritative *grand camarad*,
Step in PM, occupy this seat.
I'm tired.
What a genuine democratic practice?

Shall *petite camarad* do same?

The flowers of democracy blossomed
I call it democratic maturity,
But a syndrome of corruption set in,
That disease positioned itself,
And we lost the strength to criticize.

Generational Curses

With black, blue, Green,
Red, and purple berets,
They colour the streets of my city.
In their black and 'maron claire' boots,
Parading the street of society.
What do they do there?
Credentials they don't cross check,
Yet they pound on the innocent.

Without loud and long protest,
Without thunderous and protracted protest,
Water tanks pump on me.
Boots smash me down,
I looked up blankly,
Embraced the chilly cement cells,
As Khaki boys fell on me like bees.

Their eyes twinkled with delight,
And they smiled warmly.
I was hushed and crestfallen,
My fore head dripped with sweat,
I was nearly crying but set my teeth,
And held back my tears
To demonstrate my endurance.

My face flushed,
I looked lost in thought,
A lump came in my throat,

Tasting its bitterness in my throat,
And feeling to my very soul
I thought it's wrong.
It's a shame!
A graduate treated with disrespect?

We cherish to liberate the student folk,
Shape the tomorrow we cherish,
Plan the future we desire,
Care for the leaders of yesterday,
Nurture the leaders of today,
Shape the leaders of tomorrow,
Mould the leaders of the next generation,
Not from father to son
And avoid generational curses.

I say it unadorned

I am the man who never got ahead alone
I'm like the Man who sailed those early seas
Without a boat; without a pedal
That Man who set captives free.
Her, this is my hand; take it!

Let's form sufferer's syndicate
Set a land where every man is free
Whose sweat is acknowledged,
Whose faith and pain is not in vain,
Whose plough in the rain bears fruits

Let's bring back our mighty dream again
From our mines and forests
Send away exploiters
We must take back our land
Oh, yes, I say it unadorned,

We, the people, must use
The land, the mines, the plants, the rivers
Build our roads, bridges, railways, and dams
And construct society again
Link your hands with mine

Let's live in union as brothers
Out of that brotherhood, let power grow!
In union lies our strength.
The force that breaks yokes,
Smashes misery, crushes depression

The past has not been a bed of roses
It's of bloodshed and sorrow
But it won't last forever
That must not be today again
And not tomorrow

Out of the racks and ruins
Open new markets for farmers
Out of the mines and forests
Form new moulds, until the future blooms
To avoid a crumbling economy

We are like the bees
Full of fervent concentration
Up down, up down
From dawn to dusk
Yet live a hand to mouth life

Jumble mates

The jumble mates met once more
All day, they put out to sea
Through aquatic thoughts
When the daylight breathes its last breath
Slumber desiccated from their eyeball
They leaned on the barricade
Staring at the cockroaches
Frozen with resigned approval

Mad with the callous flies
Mosquitoes parading the room
And the manacle's malaise
On their ankles and wrists
And the damp cement floor
Turning their heads left and right
Fleeing from the boozing flies
All sighing in vain

Over jam-packed cells
Dim bulbs illuminate
Spiteful urine floors;
Stuff with inexplicable odours
Dirty and stinking in crime,
And pitiable intakes
Resigned to self-damnation
The jumble mates must succumb

They sob in anguish
With fever and headache,
Tears dropped in their hearts

A dead cold night in cold
Wondering in hurt
When "wh" questions
Pervade the echoing minds:
Why did I favour kindred?

With a gaze at on the ceiling
As if counting the number of nails
A long watch in one direction
As if in a trance
Thrashing to and fro,
Lamenting their dealings
Yet the voices of prison attendants
Might not soothe the down-cast mates?

They'll meet doom

Full of self-adulation,
Full of self-confidence,
Leaving a threatening note everywhere,
He may pick them up one by one
He may try and release them
He may try and jail them
Humiliation of the first order.

The ruler's Ministers
An absurdly qualified leadership
In an impossible age?
The ruler's dishonest cabinet
Where corruption reigns supreme
Mansions and Luxury cars surround them
Neighboured by shanty wood huts

Unelectrified huts mourn
Near where electrified gardens stand
Their endless search for pipe borne water
Can any be on the run leader?
Your watch dogs are ready.
As desperation parades distressed faces
May their own thunder strike them

It's unfortunate
They would all perish
Hawks would descend
And some devoured by vultures
So they may rot
And their bodies looted by garbage men

Yet society remains.

The Land Shall Be Ours

It was never Africa to me
As a young woman,
Full of strength, of hope,
I'll do what really needs to be done
I'll improvise, I'll do all
I fantasize about our liberty

Ready to do anything
For a continent I love
And keep a mark in society
Avoiding the same old stupid plan
No freedom in this homeland of old
There has never been its equal

I've scored a victory over tyrants
Lord, let my land be a land of freedom
One coroneted
With no false patriotic wreath,
But opportunity is real,
And life shall be free,

I'll grab the CFA, the gold, the power,
Grab the ways of satisfying needs
Not owning everything for my own greed
For honesty in work,
For honest dreams
That united we smash the old doctrine

Tasting bitterness of corruption in my throat,
Feeling to my very soul

62

Without complaining
Loud and long
I'll be the payless worker
That the mines and factories be ours

Teach new lessons,
Erase dogmas of the past
Correct every past mistake
That kept the rich enthroned
And the poor, servants
That the land might be ours,

Equality was in the air
We breathe
But that red haired man
Assumed we are of no good
And that we mutter in the dark
That we were the poor Negroes

We were tricked and pushed apart,
We are the Negro
Bearing slavery's scars
Twisted in that antique incessant chain.
We were the black men driven from home,
And they would say: Who are you that has no culture?

They Can't Hide From Judgement

We've been used and exploited,
We've been despised,
We've been rejected so many times
We've been thinking of the day of reckoning,
When they shall be standing before the judge of all.

We've been thinking how it shall be on that day,
When the present life we are living shall be rectified,
When their works shall be tasted by the boss,
When all they've done in this society shall be rewarded,
Cos they see Anglophones as inanimate.

Will the boss tell them well done?
Or depart from them?
Will he reappoint them?
Or *appelle* them to *d'autre* function?
Again I say they can't hide from Judgement

Go, go, go, les Anglos,
Do not deviate in this covenant,
Stay in my will,
Go and shine the light of Anglo-culture,
 In this crooked and perverse colonial heritage.

Stay in my will,
Doors shall be open to you,
Be vigilant, I believe we shall be accepted,
Do not exchange your dreams for money,
Do not exchange your dreams for ministerial positions.

They can't hide from God,
I've been thinking about judgement day,
Their quest for materialism and financial gain.
Eyes have not seen,
Ears have not heard,
But God knows what he shall do to them.

Time Will Heal Our Wounds

My society has sprung a leak
Military men prop up brutality
Barriers and misconceptions surround us,
We crawled from heat to fire?
Their grenades slice off citizens hands
Rendering them handicapped for life
With blood oozing from the stumps
Flowing lazily down their elbows
They run down the stream
To suck their heads in the river of peace
Then I wonder if actually we hate being called untamed.

God, give us words like Mandela.
When in his lonesome cell he spoke.
My people must learn this.
Police, Gendarme, Police…!
Remember the promise you made,
You raised up your right hand and made a vow
God, they are humans, therefore not perfect.
Speak out Lord, speak in high tones
Disperse that malicious gang,
That stands at our doors,
To paralyze our ambitions.

Like Mandela's fascinating heart,
Give my leaders spongy hearts,
To do what they want their home to be,
The land that never knew disunity.
With patience many a year I bore this.
We've heard it several times,

But it didn't strike my heart.
Are our leaders born or created?
I feel totally devastated,
But I know, time will heal our wounds,
And I'll make and remake this society.

Grenade Chopped Off My Arm

I got this half arm that I still drag,
Fighting for that same old stool.
The black beret boys and girls
Chopped off my arm
As I fight to throw back tear-gas
Held 'grenete' hard in my palm
Booooom!
It chopped off my arm

Now this riot never came to pass.
The crowd got quiet and that can of gas,
Got set aside
As they walked away
To talk about what they had done this day.
Now there's but one arm on my thorax,
You'll burn in hell
For my arm's sake.

So now it's time to decide
Which road to take,
Which one of you will follow our lead,
To stand and die
For what you believe,
For as sure as there is a rising sun,
We'll follow its rays
And God knows our course is just.

The Leader's Ministers

Full of self-adulation,
Full of self-confidence,
Leaving a threatening note everywhere,
He may pick them up one by one
He may try and release them
He may try and jail them
Humiliation of the first order.

The ruler's Ministers
An absurdly qualified leadership
In an impossible age?
The ruler's dishonest cabinet
Where corruption reigns supreme
Mansions and Luxury cars surround them
Neighboured by shanty wood huts

Unelectrified huts mourn
Near where electrified gardens stand
Their endless search for pipe borne water
Can any be on the run leader?
Your watch dogs are ready.
As desperation parades distressed faces
May their own thunder strike them

It's unfortunate
They would all perish
Hawks would descend
And some devoured by vultures
So they may rot

And their bodies looted by garbage men
And society remains.

Let Afreeka be Afreeka again

Partially in the dumps, a traumatized visage lies
Lamenting in his penal complex
Real gloom of the indignant wasteland beings
On his psyche sad words appear
Somewhere in the sands of Africa
Conveying dilemma to his sight:
Are Afreekan political leaders born to be?
Or conditioned by circumstances?

When in his vast lonely cell
Images of spirits hover
Then darkness drops again;
Fearful beast, its hour came at last
Unyielding sleep displeased by nightmares
Nightmares of Afreeka to be born
Loved in numberless forms and numberless times
In life after life, in age after age, forever.

Like M'dela's spellbound heart
I'll make and remake this society
I'm that born to be leader
From beautiful Afreeka's strand I came
In search of what I want my home to be
For I'm the one who escaped darkness
To construct a homeland of freedom
Not of animals without restrains.

For all the dreams we dream
Of all the rebellious songs we sang
Of all the hopes we held

All the freedom flags we hung
Million were shot down when we strike
Millions who had nothing as pay
I held the bodies and kissed their foreheads
And lament: Goodbye freedom fighters

Oh! Let 'Afreeka' be 'Afreeka' again
The land that's mine - the poor man's land
Afreeka, the limping giant
The land that never knew disunity
Today, the centre can no longer hold
Our dreams are almost dead today
Yet must be a land where every man is free,
And I know it will, and shall be.

I did not see the outside for years
I did not feel free air for years
For good twenty and additional five years
I couldn't plant a seed,
Couldn't recognize any root
Though I eat and shit as an adult
Clearly I was more of a baby
Only to receive and not to give

I feel for this crumbling continent
To which all error is forced:
Savage, uncivilised, dark untamed lions
This continent of love,
In whose sweating memory
Shackles of poverty, unemployment,
Hopelessness, underdevelopment, tribalism,
Corruption, nepotism, and deceit hover

I am a giant; I am that hero who'll make Afreeka
The mountains and the endless plains acknowledge
The stretches of these great green states know.
I'm an example of a sacrificial lamp
Struggling to liberate our continent
And resources from impostors
All, all if anybody asks you
Say I'm that 'Afreekan'; that leader born to be

Thwarted Hopes

We cried for help, we cried for help
Police! Police! Police! Police!
Are trying to overturn this land
We hoped for complete sovereignty
But none came; yes! None came

Barriers and misconceptions surround us
Speak in high tones my people
So the world might hear your cry
Open out from time to time
And expose those thwarted hopes

Police! Police! Police! Police!
Remember the promise you made
You raised up your right hand and made a vow
Yet trying to ruin the government
Society points accusing fingers at you all

Put your body and soul together
Dedicate part of your time
To do something that will help humanity
Something that can change somebody's life for the better
Work selflessly and leave this country a better place than you
met it

I Decry In Plain Words

Use me Lord,
Give me the rod of Moses
Let me carve up the Moungo River
I was protractedly subdued
Bizarre dealings in society
And I'll decry in plain words

They jammed me with pests
Yawning in senseless reverie
I lay on cockroaches
Surroundings I would sagaciously denounce
I could not choose but accept
I received their resolution peacefully

My people are in bondage
I pledge decline with my potency
They look much somnolent
How wash out a state?
A faction of tyrants reside there
Fault not of society but of governors

I want to cross my people
Over to a 'new world'
A 'world' bursting with concord
A 'world' gratis from marginalization
We're smooth with the Queen's tongue
A tongue not familiar with us

Use me lord, to liberate my folks.
Send us to another land

Of familiar springs and waterfalls
Now, roll your tongue in honey Lord
Articulate sweet gratifying words
They compel us to employ Napoleon's dialect

Perhaps tomorrow the earth might be gentle
Whose tears and blood watered
This land might deny us
We may not know this fatherland
Wherein our mist they now repose
Their value no tongue can tell
I decry in plain words.

Ancestors' due we can never repay
My people might loose that voice
That sang once of your tillage rose
Use me lord,
Fill me with the wrath of God
That I might instil in them the love of gentle ways.

Afreekan Poli-leaders

Variously described
Seldom in complimentary terms
Have escaped the label dictators
Claiming to be good leaders

When I was growing up,
A leader was he who leads,
Knows no tribalism,
Friendly and consoling

The reverse is really true
Uniform men pour water on citizens
Drained from toilets
To squash their demonstrations

Match from pillar to post
Choking in tear-gas and poisonous smoke
Chanting liberation songs,
They land heavy whips on their backs

My society has sprung a leak
Military men prop up brutality
Their grenades slice off innocent hands
And handicapped for life

With blood oozing from the stumps
Flowing lazily down their elbows
They run down the stream
To suck their heads in the river of peace

Afreekan people must learn this
Their Leaders, Chiefs, Fons, Lamidos,
Kings and Presidents
And that they are mortal not demi-gods

Surrender to no humanity,
Your own respect, your own dignity
Respect and honor 'big people',
All are humans, therefore not perfect

Social and economic malaise
Undermines respect and dignity
Why are we fighting each other?
Why are we trying to destroy each other?

Afreekan Poli-leaders are held accountable
With patience many a year I bore this
And today, I wonder quietly in my mind
Are African leaders born or created?

God, free us, free me like M'dela.
M'dela I understand what you went through
He stood up for what is right
Today, his people reap what he sowed

Shadowed and Ignored

I didn't choose to be a Kamaloonian
I've seen lots of faces
A shadow cast upon me
They are by my side each day
But I'm always back to you
It's crazy how I feel about you
Yet I was shadowed and ignored

I didn't choose to be born in kamaloon
I'm represented obscurely and faintly
I lie motionless in bed
You know how I feel
Each day I dream about a new Kamaloon
I went extra-mile ensuring you excel
Yet I was shadowed and ignored

As a martyr of my Country
John died running a cause
I should not be judged by my person
I should not be judged by my N double U face
I should not be judged by my S double U tongue
I am a born and bred kamaloonian
Yet I was Shadowed and ignored

Misery dominates every fibre of my being
I was trapped in a vicious cycle
Their invisible chains are stronger than we know
And of course impossible to break
I prayed to be released from burden
I managed to escape

Yet I was shadowed and ignored

The Cruelty of Tear-gas

Unhappy that the world was full of hate.
Unhappy for years of enslavement.
Unhappy for the idiots.
Unhappy for the inhumanity.

Unhappy to be part of a country full of discrimination
That treated me shoddier than it would treat a germ
Unhappy that I had to live in fear,
And in abject poverty

Unhappy that their lives were better than mine
Unhappy we've spent 50 years fighting a lost battle
Sorry for this shame of independence,
This mockery of justice,

Sorry for the cruelty of their tear-gas and granites
Their boasts of paper equality,
Their unholy licence of national greatness,
Their self-congratulation and the rejoicing,

Sorry for the hymns and sermons,
The righteous prayers to an omnipotent God,
The outright denunciation of tyrants,
The bombast, fraud, and deception,

Sorry for their thin veil of hypocrisy
Sorry for the raping,
The beating, the killing,
And the lynching of demonstrators

The savagery and years of subjugation,
Lives squandered,
Souls tortured and sent to graves
Sorry for minds and hands burned with granites.

The Bridge That Joined Us

I once crossed this river Moungo
I once sat on the Moungo Bridge
Reaching across the stretch of time
Extending my hand to touch the bridge
The skies suddenly darkened
Elements of pain swept my memory

I caught a glimpse of the river
River Moungo once changed my dreams
I once crossed this river Moungo
River, River, River,
Moungo, Moungo, Moungo
Is this the river that joined us?

I stood on the River's edge,
A weeping elephant stalk stands arms akimbo
Looking out over the water
Its eyes following the water flow
And it gracefully bends to and fro
As the South West winds beat her hair

I sat beneath the elephant stalk
I sobbed in heartbreaking grief
The elephant stalk grumbled because I sobbed;
Hopelessness and Disgruntlement
Her days are always cold
And her nights are all lonely.

Her tears dripped down from the leave's tail
Moistened the ground on which I sat,

My trouser cold to my panty
And my buttocks trembled from its embrace.
There, I sobbed and frowned
But she touched my cheek with gentle sway

Why did they bring us together?
Will they respect the terms of this marriage?
She laments because of maltreatment
She laments the wedding rights were a farce
She sobs she wasn't well educated
Yet she signed the marriage certificate.

I was a virgin from the other side of the river
Joy and sorrow, I experience both
I cannot speak *"parlé, parlé*
Yet I'm compelled to speak
I can only speak *"I was"*
But my husband rebukes me when I speak.

The Mind That Hides Within

I was angry with my mayor:
I told him my anger,
I was angry with my brothers
But I didn't tell them my anger.

I expressed my anger in fears,
Night and morning with my tears;
And they covered it with smiles,
And with soft deceitful words they caught my love.

As it grew both day and night,
Till it ended up in Foumban,
My brothers stood as witnesses
And they knew this love won't last.

Into my marital home
When the night had veiled the neighbourhood;
My husband makes his bed
My family waits to give my hand out.

Across the Moungo they sold me out
Across the Moungo they gave my hand out
Across the Moungo they throw my luggage,
And my in-laws carried me away

My husband graped my luggage and me
Opened his chambers wide apart
My very sexuality was exposed
And he coiled into me.

I didn't know I was exploited
I didn't know I was forced
I only felt his arms around me
I only felt him coil in me.

I'm not loved correctly
Deceit is the name of my love
But I'll study deep his selfish intentions
And I'll know the mind that hides within him

My people don't know
But I'll let them know:
When a woman is loved correctly
She becomes ten times
The woman she wasn't before

Ebola The Ravager

Wild Ebola, Wild Ebola
Your alarm hits Africa
Even the medical staffs too die?
Ebola your wickedness is huge
Ebola you make people fear Africa
Should I cover even my eyes?
Should I block my nostrils?
It is not airborne?
Yet it ravages my continent?

Ebola you make my mind wonder
Ebola, Ebola, Ebola
Ebola the black disease?
Is this a population reduction strategy?
Ebola you make me suspect my leaders
Ebola you divert Africa's attention
Ebola you change our theme of discussion
Ebola Africa wanted to check their records
Ebola Africa wanted to check economic failure.

A perfect storm, an African storm.
I fear an unimaginable tragedy
Since 1976 and it's now we know?
Prof Pius what can you tell Africa?
Belgian Nuns, who educated you?
Why did you use unsterilized niddles?
Kinshasa, Yambuku…!
Ebola…! The Ebola River is in trouble
You stigmatized the Ebola River

From slavery to diseases?
Wounds of cancer are still fresh
HIV / Aids still lingers
Cholera is still alive
Yellow fever and malaria is no news
Lassa fever and typhoid
And now Ebola?
Africa is a dead continent already
Ebola let old wounds heal.
Ebola give Africa peace.

Birds of the hills are singing Ebola
Frogs of the valley are croaking Ebola
The wind of the sphere is whispering Ebola
The unborn talks of Ebola
The old talk of Ebola
We are here now singing it…
Ebola Listen to this old cry for help.

Beware Africa

Ebola, Ebola, Ebola…
Ebola don do wonders
Ebola, ya own too much
Any corner for Africa na Ebola
Ebola don open Africa yi lass…
Ebola don open ma haf, haf teeth dem
Ebola you kill Africa too much…
Ebola you don finish Seria-Leon
Ebola wosai you comot?
Ebola you don come finish ma house…
Ebola wosai you comot?
Ebola dem di use you for reduce Africa?
Africa wosai we di go eh?

Ebola has done wonders
Ebola the death rate is alarming
Everywhere in Africa is Ebola
Every radio in Africa is Ebola
Every TV in Africa is Ebola
Ebola has exposed Africa
Ebola you have finished Africa
Ebola has exposed rotten tooth
Ebola do you want to terminate Seria-Leon?
Ebola where are you from?
Ebola where were you before?
Ebola you have terminated my household
Ebola where are you from?
Where are you going?
Ebola is Europe using you to reduce the African population?
Africa where are we heading too?

What a hard way to go?
What a rough way to go?

Boko Harmers

Untamed haram
Your sound hits Africa,
Kolofata est devenu votre camp? (Has Kolofata become your
camp?)
Hitting hard the Vice Prime Ministry?
Did they pay you to destroy my nation?
Boko harmers, boko harams
Trip-hammers I call you
Arms that strike in percussion
Like levers with muscular striking heads
Striking the primer in firing
Cartridges directed to the young and old
Boko haram do you fear blood?
You've lost human feelings?
Cette secte a blessé Cameroun (This sect has wounded Cameroon)
In market places
Bombs planted
Strikes the firing pin on the innocent
Hitting hard on society
Claw hammers, drop hammers
Hammer and tongs
You're nothing, but hammer mills

Sensibiliser nos progénitures
L'amour doit porter sur notre nation
Ne joindre pas les Boko Harmers
Ne prendrez pas leur argent
La population civile est en panique
L'armée camerounaise est fatigué
Lors d'intenses combats

Les soldats camerounais avaient perdu la vie.
Leave boko harmers, leave Cameroon.

The Sufferer's Syndicate

We are like bees
Full of fervent concentration
Working very hard
From dawn to dusk
Yet live a hand to mouth way of life.

I am that woman who never got ahead
I'm not that Man who sailed those early seas
Without a boat; without a pedal
I am not that Man who set captives free.
Yet I want to be His follower.

Let's form the sufferer's syndicate,
Set a land where every man is free,
Whose sweat is accredited,
Whose faith and pain is not in vain,
Whose plough in the rain bears fruits.

Let's bring back our mighty dream again,
From our mines and forests
Send away exploiters
We must take back our land again
Oh, yes, I say it plain,

People must use intelligence.
Construct society,
The land, our mines,
Link their hands with mine Lord,
That we may build our roads,
Bridges, railways, and the dams.

In union lies our strength.
The force that breaks yokes,
Smashes misery, and crushes depression
Shall we live in union as siblings?
That out of brotherhood,
Power may grow?

The past,
Not a bed of roses,
It's of bloodshed
And sorrow,
That must not be today again
And not tomorrow

Out of racks and ruins,
We'll open new markets
For farmers, miners and foresters,
Form new moulds,
Until the future blooms,
And avoid a crumbling economy.

I'll Not Judge by the Past

I looked to the lead of society,
I looked at the rear of it,
My eyes blur and ache,
In the face of confusion,
Looking through the world's frailties.
And I'll not judge by the past

This is my worry,
My heart soars,
The thought of bad becoming worse,
My heart leaps awake,
As this stares roughly at me.
And I'll not judge by the past

I stare nakedly at this world,
I stroll'd back, and stroll'd forward,
 Just as I see it, I saw it.
I know society crafted it so.
Was it like that when I was born?
And I'll not judge by the past

I tasted here, and went through there,
Tasting here and there,
Requiring freedom of personality,
But my heart is of vague impression,
And can't verbalize encouraging words.
And I'll not judge by the past

My belly rumbles, and my mind bleeds,
Society toasts people left and right.

Although I sob in recollection of the past,
I'll not judge by the past,
And perceive my folks as traitors.
And I'll not judge by the past

Their voices pull my heartstrings

It's stamped in my mind's eye,
The sight of African babes,
Confined to their huts,
Covered with moss and ferns,
Pointing to empty milk bottles,
Howling sullenly,
Utterly neglected and starving,
They make my bones weak,
Tears gush,
As their voices pull my heartstrings.

The mist curling and wandering about them,
Earthworms crawling around them,
Their feet thorn by thorns,
Unwashed and unkempt,
Full of jiggers,
Keenly requiring the soap,
And I couldn't say a word,
As my soul took form,
Tears gush,
As their voices pull my heartstrings.

Melancholy

The masters' baby has had milk,
Bebelac, nutricia and berger.
Their dogs too have had enough,
Their flower gardens all watered,
The gateman's baby screams for crumbs,
The yard man's baby screams for left-overs,
Its dog wagging its tail
Begging for bones,
Even flies too scramble on oily plates,
Yet, Madam scolds at them.

Curling up themselves in the wood ashes,
Mosquitoes sucking them up,
May God convict the white jacket men,
They sold their mosquito nets,
Protecting instead, those who have insecticides,
Disregarding the have-nots,
The rich get richer,
And the moneyed ones get well-off;
May the powers that be, look for their whips
Because vulnerable voices pull my heartstrings.

My eyes followed them,
Flies swag around them,
Sitting on the ground,
On bare floor and bare buttocks,
In an attitude of grief and debasement,
Gulping from grubby kettles,
Eating but little food,
Of a coarse kind,

Tears gush,
As their voices pull my heartstrings.

Seraph

The sob of Seraph twirls my psyche,
The cry on her lips wounded my soul,
A shrouded figure in garbage,
Close to the thrash can she stands,
With her running nostrils,
Unkempt hair,
Watching the cans overflow so grand,
Seeking for that to have as milk.

The sob of Seraph twirls my psyche,
An Angel in silence,
Standing motionless in gloom,
Without her toys and joy,
With watered-down cheeks,
Like a stream of water,
Shivering and Unable to speak her name,
As she sips a filthy stream of water.

The sob of Seraph twirls my psyche,
With a head full of contemplation,
I lowered myself to the ground,
I felt the cold and dark atmosphere,
I smelled the scent of pity,
Calling for paper columns;
Though I weep, I'll make my feelings felt,
And my pen shall not run short of ink.

The sob of Seraph twirls my psyche,
I stretched my compassionate hand,
To steal a feel of her cold self,

But like the airstream,
Without my grasp,
She whirled on, escaping my clasp,
Enveloped herself in hurtful wire,
Leaving my spirit cheerless and dejected

The sob of Seraph twirls my psyche.
Arise law makers of our land,
Stretch that Charity hand,
That conciliates distressed minds,
So you would get to understand,
To listen to the cry of every man,
Listen to Seraph's infant's cry of fear,
And bring the happiness Seraph can barely find.

I am A Nobody

Sure, call me any horrible name you choose,
The ugly name does not stain.
I am the poor Anglo-fool,
Fooled and pushed apart.
I am like a slave bearing drudger scars.
Submitting to a dominating influence,
And finding only the same old stupid plan.

I am the Anglo-fool driven from the land.
I am the young Anglo-fool, full of strength and hope.
I am the Anglo-fool clutching the hope I seek,
But tangled in that ancient endless chain,
Forced to move like that ancient slave,
And so my fist is clenched,
Determined to take back my freedom again.

It's a shame!
I am the Anglo-fool, belittled.
I am the Anglo-fool sold to the French.
I am the Anglo-fool, servant to Franco-fools.
Owning everything for your own greed?
The bartered citizen throughout the years?
Yet I'm one of those who dreamt our indispensable dream?

I am the man who never gets ahead.
Oh! I'm the man who sailed those early seas in the Biafra,
In search of what I meant to be my independence.
With my bricks and stones, I gave a helping hand,
To build a "free Cameroon."
I am one of them that dreamt a dream so strong,

So brave, so true
Yet I am a nobody.

Gray Tears

Sparkling coiled as they spurt
They were those grey hairs
Old and very skinny
Exposed chest bones
Empty front row of teeth
Trembling fingers and hands
Soft and succulent palms
Like those of a two day old
That grey haired man wept

Endeavours to greet
Adjusting his lenses
He rises up his head
As to the Heavens
He takes a glance at me
1884 marked the beginning of this mess?
It is a huge History
Sometimes in violence and bloodshed
Speaking in a voice like a stream
And I looked at him in tremor

He attempts a mourning but blocked smile
No word could I decipher
He spoke in an almost whisper,
The First World War, the war
His voice trembled in gray tears
His shape and all baffles
With an amputated arm
The remains of warfare
And he wore silver bracelets

His eyes and eyeballs all grey
Wisdom inscribed on him
I tickled him to speak
At last! He swaggers
In a shrill voice he spoke
"Oh! I'll expose them
I see doom, I see misery
I grieve for the guiltless
The struggle for independence continues.

Be honest, be truthful
Touch not the state purse
See the innocent suffering
Languishing in detention centres
Accusing fingers tip at them
The cement floor will be your bed too
That man looks for victims
Exercise loyalty, be trustworthy
You're all burglars.

Johnny's Walk Too Foumban

Small John showed the way
We arrived Foumban in ignorance
We flee from the devil
And embraced an unknown Angel?
Johnny did not educate us
And we accepted Alahaji's proposal
Like cockroaches we ran away from the heat of fire
And fell in a pot of hot oil
It was a cool adventure.

Our greatest bullet is the power of our confidence
Taking our destiny into our own hands.
It was like a choice between cancer and AIDs
Join Nigeria or join the Independent 'La Reuplique?
It was like running from a roaring lion
Just to embrace a hungry tiger
We are decision takers far from making decisions
No seat on the decision table
It was a cool adventure

Some sacrificed their lives,
That we might become responsible for our own deeds.
But our opinions don't count.
Today, we are 'les Anglos'
'Les gens de Johnny"
'Les Bamenda, les Kumba'
Allez mangez vos 'eru', vos 'achu'
We need voices of freedom
Courageous and incorruptible breeds

Be determined to act as courageous citizens
We have experienced misery
Depression, wretchedness and melancholy
In spite of your suffering, don't give up
We need a critical mass
A mass that will intelligently gaze
Into the future and shade light
Victory, is for those who endure
And not for those who quit.

I Swear To This Oath

For all the dreams we've dreamed
And all the songs we've sung
And all the hopes we've held
And all the flags we've hung,
We'll have nothing to show forth
But the almost dead dream.

For the thousands unemployed today
For the thousands shot down when we strike
For the thousands who have nothing to eat?
For the thousands who have nothing to show for?
Yet I swear this oath,
I'll die a Cameroonian.

I say it plain, I'll show the way
This Land ought to be as I desire
We'll look up to Him for mercy
We'll look onto his Jeremiah words
And will not stop looking
Unless He withdraws his words

I Will Carve Up the Moungo

They jammed me with pests
Yawning in senseless reverie
I lay on cockroaches
Surroundings I would sagaciously denounce
I could not choose but accept
I received their resolution peacefully

Bizarre deal in society
Use me Lord,
Give me the rod of Moses
Let me carve up the Moungo River
I was protractedly subdued
And I'll decry in plain words

My people are in bondage
I pledge decline with my potency
They look much somnolent
How wash out a state?
A faction of tyrants reside there
Fault not of society but of governors

I want to cross my people
Over to a 'new world'
A 'world' bursting with concord
A 'world' gratis from marginalization
We're smooth with the Queen's tongue
A tongue not familiar with us

Use me lord, to liberate my folks.
Send us to another land

To familiar springs and waterfalls
Now, roll your tongue in honey Lord
Articulate sweet gratifying words
They compel us to employ Napoleon's dialect

Perhaps tomorrow the earth might be gentle
Whose tears and blood watered
This land might deny us
We may not know this fatherland
Wherein our mist they now repose
Their value no tongue can tell
And I decry in plain words.

Ancestors' due we can never repay
My people might lose that voice
That sang once of your tillage rose
Use me lord,
Fill me with the wrath of God
That I might instil in them the love of gentle ways.

Pain In My Siesta

Pain in my siesta
In each dream I see it again
I tell pain to dislocate
Sometimes it does but comes back again,
Sometimes I sleep as if my pain is not with me
But then it comes again when I begin slumber
My pain is my number one enemy
Hitherto it is with me everywhere I go
And I do not know how to make it go away completely?

Is pain my spouse?
I used to love my sound sleep
But now I sleep with pain
Pain that takes much of the pleasure away
And I'm in all shackles
I wonder if it will be pain for the rest of my life
Or whether somehow something will get me out of it
Pain overwhelms my soul
And my world filled with shame

Ancestral Tears

The long nose man came,
With big book
And big Bible,
Bringing a brutal civilisation,
Yearning for victims,
Destroying sweet laughter,
Bringing contempt
And abhorrence.

Africa,
Dear fatherland,
It knew no decay, no hatred
Solidarity, hospitality
Conviviality reigned,
We drank from one spring,
But today, today it's in ruins,
Of war, violence and hatred

My ancestors battled in vain,
It was a nightmare to my people,
A real nightmare
And battlefield,
Under the yoke of evangelisation,
Coarse manners,
Vulgar expressions,
And deformities of wrangled lives.

Although ancestors weep,
That white skin man insisted,
Bringing disunity,

Calamity and destruction
Claiming it civilisation,
A very brutal Civilisation,
Overshadowing peace
In a once peaceful people.

That man uprooted them
Ancestral trees,
Ancestral heads
Frightened by whips,
My people succumb,
My grandfather's grave was moved,
And he planted his God,
Bringing in disrespect for tradition

In nature I'll walk,
Walking in the global village,
I'll make my presence felt,
In a typical African spirit,
I'll lift up my *nkeng* leaves,
I'll spray my cam wood
And I'll show the world
That peace and harmony reigns in Africa

The Revolver in African Arms

Africa, Africa, Africa,
Where are we heading to?
Africa, wosai we di go?
War here, conflict there?
Quel est l'avenir de vos enfants?
Kenya, Central Africa and Congo;
Dead bodies lying helplessly,
So motionless,
And their eyes stare unblinking
Yet the revolver is in African Arms

Women sing lullabies
To cheerless and crying babies,
Sad, sad melodies some produce,
A sign of distress I say.
The green, thick leaves die and fall away,
The birds too stop singing,
For they too are dying.
Even the air is still,
For nothing grows anymore
Yet the revolver is in African Arms

Independence brings harmony,
Reconciliation and riches;
Yet Africa is underdeveloped.
We've become beggars in the world,
We've been termed the poor,
And heavily indebted.
We've become a cry baby in the world,
Our hands always stretched,

Begging for salvation
Yet the revolver is in African Arms

African leaders, let us unite

Break down all barriers,
Stop fighting, killing and corruption
Plant the seeds of unity, tolerance and love.
Let's wave the flag of peace,
It's time to exchange guns for medicine
Our weapon should be moral education
Let our pens replace spears,
Bows and arrows
Let the Bible be our sole weapon

I shall move into the global village,
Then In a typical African spirit,
I shall lift up the peace plant,
Remove my calabash,
And spray cam wood in Africa.
I'll give a red card to war zones.
We must stop war in Africa!!!!!
Harmony must reign in Africa

In A Predicament All My Life

Rio dos cameroes!
It was the river of prawns,
A cruel dream,
Men sold and shipped,
It was at Bimbia.
The slave trade zone
Dikolo chiefdom harboured them.
And they took us as prisoners
With chains around our feet
Les blanches, les blanches
Vous nous à tromper beaucoup
Shall I be in a predicament all my life?

We toil every day
We were worked in hot sun
Until tears and sweet stain their cheeks
The master gains
And we suffer.
They came with the Bible,
Invaded Africa in all nooks,
And crannies,
Alfred Saker came with them too,
Those men ended barbarism
Were they European powers in search of space?
They only opened bribery and corruption.
Shall I be in a predicament all my life?

My tears drop because they don't know
I've lost all in reunification
I showed them true love

Look at what they've done to me
You cried to me,
I gave you all the morals
Now you call me in the face a fool?
I'm helpless without your care,
And it's hurting to know how I feel
Yesterday I worked for independence
Now they talk of independence
Please show us the thoughts of your mind
Shall I be in a predicament all my life?

They live in the GRA,
Electrified homes,
Even the lawns too electrified.
Their dogs eat and throw up
We die in misery
Yet we work hard every day.
I'm angry, and I'll protest
I'm marching
I want to change this country
I shall not be a beggar all day
We'll prefer crayfish in freedom
Than chew chicken in servitude,
Now, I'm in a predicament all my life.

Tear-Drop s In My heart

For minutes, days and incessant months,
You walk away and not returning,
I sit and wonder every day what I did wrong.
You told me you loved me
I missed the smiles at Foumban
Why did it have to end?
After a long struggle
When we start reaping our fruits?
I wait for you at super
On a table set for two
You kept a distance'
And you call me names?

I wonder why I love you
Why did you accept reunification?
Today you reap what we both sowed
And everything we both planted
We planned to walk a little faster
We planned to have some fun
I'm hurt because of what you've done
Come take my hand
Tears drop in my heart
Give back the missing piece in me
You are my missing piece
Please show me the love you promised

I guess I've complained too much,
I feel ignored when I scream for help
I told you I'll never leave you
I kept my promise but you didn't

Everyday I have to pretend
I have to fake a smirk
I have to fake a laugh
I have to fake all
Fooling myself
Saying all is fine
Just to conceal how I feel
Yet tears drop in my heart

Why I Hate Boko Harams

What the future holds,
I do not know
I ponder my thoughts; here as I sit
My thoughts drift in and out of me
Like a movie, I see them so clear.

I have lost loved ones along the way
I carry them in my heart everyday
I hate the way they lay motionless
I hate the way they their lives ended
And I hate when the Boko Harams stare.

I hate your big guns and combat boots
And the way you raid my home
I hate the boko harams
I hate their ways,
They make me sick

They even make me rime
I hate the way they kill innocent citizens
I hate it when they break houses unannounced
I hate it when they make me sad
Even worse when they make me cry.

I hate it when they destroy life
I hate the way they demolish buildings
Shut up now, Boko Haram, don't say a word
Unspoken thoughts, I've already had
We can't recover tracks it's too late

We Will Survive the Hurt

People survive wars
People survive disasters
People survive accidents
People survive sadness
People survive hurt
People survive people
People survive segregation
So, why wouldn't we?

We've always provided cold water
We've always treated them fairly
We smiled when they smile
We weep when they mourn
We've always loved them
We've always treated them as kindred
Our brothers East the Moungo
But right now, they offer us vinegar

Right now,
Our brothers across the bridge
They make our cheeks wet
When we think of them
Our hearts broke
Our sorrows grows
Our pains grow more
Our disillusionment comes back.

In sorrowfulness
When their lives were a nightmare

And they soaked their cheeks with tears
We offered them our shoulders
We borrowed them our handkerchiefs
Our cloth ends were wet
Our feet covered with mud
And we drip in sorrow

With our faces towards the sun
We'll be among them
Those people to survive pain
A voice inside keeps pampering us
We try not to cry
We try not to sob
Though our hearts sink,
We'll survive the pain

We'll expose them
Our pens have ink
We have to write these stanzas
To remind ourselves,
Our listeners
And our readers
Sometimes how it is,
How sad it is when you live with scorpions

All is Vanity

It's deplorable
To see the vanity of it,

He who has set his heart upon the world,
So that evil can be well rooted.

Wish they have enough knowledge
Enough virtue to despise all vanity

I'll expose every bit as I can
They're like pretty thieves.

Those that cheat the innocent perhaps
Pick pockets in the mist of company

Just a tiny word from Heaven
Can disarm them

I have time on my hands
To air my opinion

All earthly things are vanity
Oh! Yes! Vanity

The Raided Northern Cameroon

Boko Haram,
Mounting fears
Boko Haram,
Suicide bombing

Your perfume suffocates
Your foot steps
Tremble the earth
So too are your boots

Your armours
Your helmets
Your bullets
Your guns frighten Cameroonians.

Leave Amchide alone
Leave the North alone
The Tourou area is in chaos
Even the rats too flee from you?

You torch houses
You knock doors
You carry away the guiltless
Women and innocent children

Even the blameless insects?
Kidnappers!
Boko Haram!
Who are Boko Harams?

Haram Assaults

Dreadful Insurgents
Evil, evil people
Civilians massacred
For wealth or fame?

They launched an operation
They burn down abodes
They torch hiding places
Dreadful insurgents

The Boko haram
The bomber
Life means nothing to you?
Humans executed like animals?

Boko haram,
Haram assaults
Aggravated assaults
You use assault boats?

You use assault rifle
What shall it profit you?
Why do you take lives?
What shall you gain at the expense of life?

Why have you sold your soul to devil?
God, advance towards this
Haram assaults
Must reap what they sow.

Printed in the United States
By Bookmasters